Prince William

The Story So Far

Written by Michael Johnstone

A Funfax Book

Prince William
The Story So Far

Copyright © 1999 Funfax Ltd.
Woodbridge, Suffolk, IP12 1AN, England.
All rights reserved.

DK Australia
PO Box 414
St. Leonards
NSW 1590
Australia

DK Publishing, Inc.
95 Madison Avenue
New York, NY 10016

Key: t = top; b = bottom; c = centre

All Action 8, 9, 13, 33, 47, Mark Cuthbert 26, 48,
Alan Davidson 10, Gareth Davies 27, Anwar Hussein 6, 36, 39, 41, 44,
Doug Peters 1, Duncan Radan 18, Jez C. Self 14, Paul Smith 12
Rex Features 9, 16, 19, 24, 25, 38, Jim Bennett 32, 40, 42, 43, 46,
James Grey 7, David Hartley 30, 37,
Jeff Jefferson 4, 5, 8b, 23, C. Postlethwaite 21,
Orgensen/Rooke 45, Tim Rooke 1, 3, 8t, 14, 29, 34, 35
The Sun 22
Today 12, 20
Front cover James Grey

Full name:	William Arthur Philip Louis Mountbatten-Windsor
Date of birth:	June 21, 1982
Weight at birth:	7 lb. 10 oz. (3.46 kg)
Star sign:	Gemini
Current residences:	Eton College, Eton; St. James's Palace, London; Highgrove House, Gloucestershire
Height:	6 ft. 2 in. (1.88 m)
Parents:	HRH, The Prince of Wales, and Diana, Princess of Wales (formerly Lady Diana Spencer)
Hair:	Dark blond
Eyes:	Blue
Nicknames:	Wombat, King Tot, Basher, Wills
Pinups:	Pamela Anderson, Cindy Crawford, Claudia Schiffer, Baby Spice

Dislikes:	Being photographed
Best quality:	Always willing to take the initiative
Bad habits:	Ignores people he doesn't trust, and takes himself too seriously
Likes to eat:	Burgers, pizza, venison, and chocolate
Likes to drink:	Coke
Likes to watch:	*Baywatch*
Likes to listen to:	Pulp, Spice Girls, and Jon Bon Jovi
Best sports:	Swimming, skiing, and shooting
Pets:	Labrador called Widgeon
Little-known fact:	He's left-handed

London, September 6, 1997

As the gun carriage carrying the coffin of Diana, Princess of Wales, stopped between Trafalgar Square and Buckingham Palace in London, three men and two boys joined the funeral procession as it continued its journey to Westminster Abbey. The men were Diana's ex-husband, The Prince of Wales; her former father-in-law, the Duke of Edinburgh; and her brother, the Earl Spencer. The boys were her sons, Prince Harry, nearly 13, and Prince William, aged 15.

With television cameras from almost every country in the world focused on him, his head bowed and his fair hair flowing over his brow, William won the sympathy of countless hearts around the world.

Greenwich, England, November 1997

Guests waiting for the royal party to arrive at a lunch to celebrate the golden wedding anniversary of the Queen and the Duke of Edinburgh were surprised to hear screams coming from outside. Police on duty were taken aback by the noise. Clapping and cheers were the usual way that crowds greeted the Royal Family. But screams? It turned out that they were for William. "He's becoming quite a pinup," a member of the Royal Family joked later.

Vancouver, British Columbia, March 1998

Before setting off for a private skiing holiday, the Prince of Wales stopped in Vancouver to attend a few public engagements with William and Harry, who had been more or less out of the public eye for six months.

The naturally shy, young Prince William was not fond of public appearances. When he had arrived in Canada, William had adopted his normal technique when he knows the cameras are on him—head down, gazing at the ground in front of him, walking as quickly as possible, just as his mother did when she found the press overattentive. It was a different William who emerged a day or two later to greet some of the teenage girls waiting outside the hotel where the royal party was staying.

It had been his father's idea. "Chat to a few of them," he told his nervous son. "Shake some hands. And remember to smile." Blushing, William walked over to the lines of girls and followed his father's advice. He shook hands, answered questions, smiled—and set countless hearts beating faster and faster. William was sociable, courteous, and, in the words of one of the girls there, "drop-dead gorgeous." Another agreed. "He's rich, he's gorgeous, and he's a prince. What more do you need?" she said.

Later, when photographs showed the prince smiling, laughing, and wearing a bomber jacket and baseball cap, it was obvious that a new royal superstar had been born.

Princess Diana had refused to have her baby in Buckingham Palace. Instead, Prince William was born on June 21, 1982, in the private wing of St. Mary's Hospital. Diana, 13 years younger than her husband, wanted to call her son one of the popular names of her generation—Sebastian was said to be the one she liked most. A traditionalist, Charles wanted to call his heir Albert, after Queen Victoria's husband, and after his own grandfather, who had taken the title King George VI when he had come to the throne in 1936.

On August 4, the boy was christened William Arthur Philip Louis, in the Music Room at Buckingham Palace, by the Archbishop of Canterbury. William had an impressive array of godparents, including King Constantine II (the deposed King of Greece), Princess Alexandra (the Queen's first cousin), and the Duchess of Westminster (the wife of one of Britain's wealthiest men).

Almost from the beginning, the baby was known to his family as Wills. Whenever their royal duties allowed them time off, Charles and Diana could be found in the nursery playing with Wills, bathing and changing him. And when he was ill, Diana slept beside him until he was better. Even from the start, the bond between Diana and William was destined to be exceptionally strong.

There's an old photograph of a very young Prince Charles welcoming his mother back from a state visit. No hug. No kiss. Instead, a very serious little boy shaking hands with the mother he hadn't seen for several weeks. In contrast, there's some famous television footage of Princess Diana returning to the royal yacht *Britannia*, while on a state visit to Canada. She's running along the gangplank, arms outstretched and whooping with joy to embrace William and Harry (her second son, born in 1984).

*D*iana decided from the very beginning that the traditional way of bringing up royal children was not for William and Harry. There were to be no governesses. Instead, when he was three, William went to Mrs. Mynor's nursery school in West London. After two years, he was sent to Wetherby School, a day school in Kensington, where he stayed for three years before going to boarding school, Ludgrove, in Berkshire. As often as she could, Diana drove Wills to school and picked him up in the afternoon. At sports days, Diana stood on the side cheering Wills (and later Harry) on, and didn't hesitate to kick off her shoes and compete in the mothers' race.

Charles hoped that when Wills finished at Ludgrove, he would follow in his footsteps and go to Gordonstoun, in the Highlands of Scotland. Much later, Charles admitted that he had hated his years there. However, his brothers Andrew and Edward had relished the tough outdoor regime. Charles hoped his children would find the Gordonstoun experience exhilarating as well as educational.

*I*t was while he was in Australia that Wills took his first swim. With water wings attached to his arms, he splashed happily around in the pool at Woomargama. Wills must have enjoyed the experience, as he is now one of the top 100 swimmers for his age in the 50 m freestyle, and winner of Eton's 1997 Junior 50 and 100 m freestyle.

It was also in Australia that Wills got into his first scrape. Dragging a lace tablecloth off a table, he sent the cups and saucers and a plate of cookies crashing to the floor. His natural curiosity got him into trouble again a few months later at Balmoral, the Queen's castle in Scotland, where she and the Royal Family spend their summer holidays. Left on his own for a minute or two, he spotted a button on the nursery wall. There was no way he could have known that when it was pushed, an alarm was triggered in Aberdeen's police headquarters several miles away. Naturally he pushed it, and within seconds police from all over the Highlands were racing to Balmoral, which they sealed off while they searched the grounds for a would-be assassin. When they realized it was William who had set the alarm off, Nanny Barnes was terribly embarrassed; Diana, on the other hand, could hardly contain her giggles.

She found it funny, too, when Wills took to putting anything he could lay his hands on down the toilet and then flushing it. Charles usually laughed too, but he was a little upset when he found the toddler trying to flush away Charles's shoes. Some parents may have gently corrected their children for these and other mischievous antics. But Charles and Diana were charmed by their son, whom they had nicknamed "Wombat."

William

When William was 19 months old, Diana discovered that she was going to have another baby. Three months after his second birthday, Wills was taken to see his day-old baby brother for the first time. He obviously loved his little brother Harry from the very start, and tried to pick him up and play with him whenever he could. He even attempted to do this at Harry's christening at Windsor Castle, the Queen's home in Berkshire. After the ceremony, when the royal party posed for television cameras, millions of television viewers saw young William ignoring everyone, even the Queen, as he tried to get his way.

By now, even Prince Charles was forced to admit that Wills's conduct was becoming a problem, but Diana and Nanny Barnes both doted on the boy, and they were reluctant to discipline him. It

wasn't until Wills had run riot at a family gathering, and had started being rude to servants, that Diana agreed that Wills was getting far too boisterous. The solution was to send him to a nursery school, where he could mix and play with other children of his own age. After a long search, Diana settled on Mrs. Mynor's school in Notting Hill Gate, not far from Kensington Palace, where the Wales's lived.

Well aware that the press would be there to snap photographs of William at every opportunity, the Prince and Princess wrote to the editors of every major British newspaper, asking them to let him attend school in peace after the first day, when the press and television cameras would be welcome. Some 150 cameras clicked as William quite calmly made his way up the steps into the school.

*E*ven though he was just three, William was not afraid to pull rank on the 35 other children to get his own way. "If you don't do what I want, I'll have you arrested," he would say. And if that didn't work, he was not afraid to resort to physical force, which resulted in many scraps between him and his classmates. His mother was very embarrassed when she learned what had happened when one of Wills's classmates had his birthday party at school. William had refused to sit with the other children, threw his food on the floor, and when ordered to clean up the mess he told the staff, "When I'm king, I'm going to send all my knights round to kill you." Nickname number two—King Tot!

At home, William was turning into a cheeky, stubborn little boy, refusing to do what he was told. Even in public, William misbehaved. At Prince Andrew's wedding to Sarah Ferguson, when Wills was a page boy, the bride's other attendants all behaved perfectly. Not William. He fidgeted all the time, and stuck his tongue out at the bridesmaids. He also had a habit of pinching women's bottoms. Diana thought it was hilarious when he pinched hers, but when he started pinching the bottoms of maids and girlfriends who came to visit her at Kensington Palace, and worse—when he pinched a woman's bottom at a school sports day—Diana had to tell him to stop.

A year after William had disgraced himself at his Uncle Andrew's wedding, he left Mrs. Mynor's school to go to Wetherby—a pre-prep school close to Kensington Palace. Pre-prep schools are attended by children who are destined to be sent off to their first boarding school, or prep school, when they are seven or eight. A few months before he started at Wetherby, Nanny Barnes—who Prince Charles had come to believe was far too soft with Wills—left. She was replaced by Ruth Wallace, or "Nanny Roof" as Wills and Harry called her, who was much stricter than Nanny Barnes had been.

*H*er influence was soon noticeable in the change in the way William behaved. The Prince and Princess gave Nanny Roof permission to smack the boys, and with his new school keen to teach pupils good manners, William's conduct improved. He still got into scrapes at school, as most young children do. He could fire his water pistol with unnerving accuracy, something that stood him in good stead when his father taught him how to handle a shotgun. He was also a reckless tree-climber, and on several occasions he had to be guided down from branches over 50 feet above the ground!

When he was at Wetherby, Nanny Roof would wake William up at 7:30 a.m., help him to wash and change into his school uniform, and serve him and Harry breakfast. Unless their parents were abroad or out of London on public duties, the two boys always saw their mother and father before setting off for school. If she could, Diana drove them to school herself and tried to be home to read them a bedtime story and kiss them goodnight.

Goodnight kisses, during the school year at least, came to an end for William in 1990, when he was sent to Ludgrove Preparatory School in Berkshire. Any boy who goes to prep school is terrified that his mother will let him down and cry in public. So imagine how William must have felt when, after shaking hands with his new headmaster and being shown around the school, it was time to say goodbye to his parents. William was serious but calm; Princess Diana reached for the tissues and burst into tears.

By the time William went to Ludgrove, it was obvious that his parents' marriage was in trouble—not to members of the public, who remembered Diana and Charles's fairy-tale romance, engagement, and wedding in 1981, but to friends of the couple, members of the Royal Family, and many journalists, who were aware that Charles and Diana had grown further and further apart since the birth of Prince Harry. Just three years later, in 1987, Charles had moved all his personal belongings out of Kensington Palace. Shortly afterward, he moved his office to Highgrove.

On his first week-long break from Ludgrove, William burst into his father's office, desperate to see "Papa." Charles wasn't there; he had gone to Balmoral, where he was enjoying an autumn break. William burst into tears. Diana immediately called her husband and asked him to fax William a welcome-home message, the first of many faxed messages between father and son. It was not that Charles was an uncaring father—he adored his sons—but he had been brought up to believe that duty comes first. When William fractured his skull after being hit on the head with a golf club, Charles, after making sure that his son would recover, continued a visit to the Royal Opera House the same evening.

After he moved his private office to Highgrove, Charles rarely spent a night in London unless he had to, preferring the countryside and the companionship of an old girlfriend, Camilla Parker Bowles. Diana, who was battling against bulimia nervosa (an eating disorder), preferred London. She loved shopping and enjoyed gossiping with friends in fashionable restaurants. However, most Friday afternoons she forced herself to drive to Highgrove after picking up Wills (and later Harry) from school, so that they could see their father for the weekend.

The two boys had adored going to Highgrove when they were little. It was here where they learned to ride horses, where they climbed trees and spent time on the estate farm, knowing there was no chance of prying photographers and their cameras. Now it was different. Charles and Diana found it difficult to be in each other's company, even for the sake of their two boys. Meals were eaten in silence, and as soon as he could, Charles would head for the garden, leaving Diana to entertain the children.

It was different during the holidays, when Wills and Harry could be at Kensington Palace. Then Diana would take them to Alton Towers, the famous theme park, where she and her sons were photographed munching burgers and fries like any other happy family. Only their father wasn't there.

$\mathcal{T}$here were outings to watch tennis and the movies, trips to Disney World, and holidays abroad, often in the Caribbean. Then, when Diana would return to London, the young princes would join their father in England or Scotland.

It's bad enough for "ordinary" children when their parents' marriages go through bad patches, but at least they can brave their misery in private. But not long after Wills went to Ludgrove, more and more stories about his parents' marriage began to

appear. The staff at Ludgrove tried to shield William from the newspaper stories, but fellow pupils told their parents that the prince could often be seen by himself, wandering aimlessly around the school grounds, looking as if all the cares in the world were on his young shoulders. He knew his parents loathed each other. When they were together, furious arguments would erupt. After one dispute, when Diana had locked herself in the bathroom, William pushed some tissues under the door with a note saying, "Don't cry Mummy." And after another awful quarrel, when he was just seven, he picked up the telephone and booked a table for himself and Diana at San Lorenzo—a chic restaurant in London's fashionable Beauchamp Place, where the princess enjoyed eating.

On March 1, 1991, William undertook his first official engagement—unveiling a plaque in Cardiff, the capital city of Wales. Wearing a daffodil for Wales's patron saint, he shook hands, blushing when a little girl presented him with flowers, and more deeply when an older woman gave him a kiss. At one point, he turned to his mother and asked how much longer this was going to last. Princess Diana may well have been tempted to say, "All your life."

Knowing there's more to being a king than unveiling plaques and shaking hands, Diana wanted William and Harry to

learn about the underprivileged with whom she had created a special bond—the homeless, sufferers from AIDS, and drug addicts. During school holidays, the Princess arranged for her sons to accompany her on private visits to meet such people. "I want William and Harry," she said, "to experience what most people already know; that they are growing up in a multiracial society in which everyone is not rich or has four holidays a year, or speaks standard English and drives a Range Rover."

Just before Christmas in 1992, when William was ten and Harry eight, it was announced that the Prince and Princess of Wales were to separate. The day before the announcement was made, Diana drove to Ludgrove to tell William. When she had finished, William kissed her on the cheek and said, "I hope you will both be happier now."

The separation didn't change William's life much, although he found that Christmas—the first one away from his mother, when he joined the rest of the Royal Family at Sandringham—particularly hard. Outside of school, he continued to divide his time between Kensington Palace and Highgrove. In London, Diana took the boys to the movies and burger bars, and allowed them to dress in jeans and T-shirts—not the suits, shirts and ties, and highly polished shoes they wore when they accompanied their father in public.

Prince Charles is a countryman at heart; he loves shooting, fishing, hunting, and stalking deer. It was really only when he started to teach Wills these skills, that the boy saw how relaxed his father was and what good fun he could be. It was different indoors, especially if the Queen was present. Then William had to behave impeccably: wait until he was spoken to before he could speak, dress elegantly, and remember how he should address everyone.

At Kensington Palace, William and Harry could make as much noise as they wanted, race along corridors, and watch as much television as they liked. They met Diana's friends: James Hewitt, a young cavalry officer who helped teach William to ride, and Will Carling, captain of England's triumphant rugby team. Later, when Hewitt cooperated in a book about his relationship with Diana, and Carling and his wife separated because of his friendship with the Princess, William believed that both men had betrayed her.

Just before Easter in 1993, a new woman entered William's life, when his father employed Victoria Legge-Bourke. Officially an assistant to Charles's private secretary, and nicknamed "Tiggy" because of her love of Beatrix Potter's Mrs. Tiggywinkle, she was unofficially given the job of helping look after the boys.

William soon came to think of Tiggy as a big sister, and she, Harry and Wills would enjoy pillow fights in their bedrooms, games of soccer, and ducking each other in the pool. The boys thought it was wonderful when she taught them how to shoot rabbits, and William especially confided in her and looked to her for advice.

Reports were soon appearing in the papers that Diana was furious and jealous of her sons' relationship with Tiggy. When the Princess was rude to the younger woman at the Christmas party the Wales's threw for their staff at a London hotel, the papers reported the story with glee. William couldn't understand his mother's attitude. There was no reason for her to be so jealous; he adored his mother and nobody, no matter how much fun they were, could ever take her place.

Despite his parents' sour relationship with each other, William enjoyed his years at Ludgrove. He made friends, was an eager pupil, and was good at sports—especially soccer. His aggression on the playing field, and sometimes off it, earned him his third nickname, "Basher." He loved the fact that at school there were no photographers around to catch him off guard, as there were so often when he was spending the weekend in London with his mother. The only thing that irritated William about school was the constant presence of his private detectives, and with the help of friends he would sometimes try to lose them. His father was forced to put a stop to this, explaining that the men were only doing their jobs, although the prince arranged for the men to remain out of sight as much as possible.

*D*uring his final year, when he was made a prefect (student monitor), he passed his common entrance—the academic tests that all children going to private schools must take. Three months after his 13th birthday, Prince William became the first male heir to the throne to enter Eton—Britain's most famous private school.

Outside of school, he became friends with his father's cousin, Viscount Linley, who is the motorcycle-riding son of his great-aunt, Princess Margaret, and with his own cousin, Peter Philips, Princess Anne's sporty elder child. The fact that both of these young men came from broken marriages and understood the torment William had been through created a strong bond between them.

The all-boys school, founded by Henry VI in 1440, is very traditional. But if William was nervous when he arrived there with both his parents and his little brother to sign the register, he didn't show it. Possibly the fact that many of his school friends from Ludgrove were to join William at Eton helped to soothe away any first-day nerves. It was a very confident young teenager who stepped out of the gates of Manor House wearing the unique Eton uniform—dark tail coat, waistcoat and pinstripe trousers, stiff white collar, and white bow tie.

The ivy-covered Manor House is the home of William and 49 other Eton boys. William, like all Etonians, has a personal tutor who oversees his academic progress and general development, including the choice of sports to be played. William chose soccer, rowing, and, later, swimming. He had a huge choice of subjects to choose from, from Mandarin Chinese and mechanics, to ancient Greek and art, which William is excellent at—obviously inheriting his father's talent as a painter. Pupils are expected to excel at whatever they do, and the atmosphere is intensely competitive— something many youngsters, including William, find hard to adapt to at first.

William, like all other boys at Eton, has his own small study-bedroom. The only concessions to his royal status are the fact that he has a private bathroom and is called by his first name. His ever-present bodyguard sleeps nearby. It's against the rules to stick posters on the walls, but pinups are allowed inside locker doors. To date, pop star Baby Spice, models Claudia Schiffer and Cindy Crawford, and *Baywatch* belle Pamela Anderson have smiled on Wills when he opens his locker door.

When school is over for the day, William is free to roam the streets of Eton and Windsor with his friends, wearing casual clothes—chinos, denim shirts, baggy sweaters, and deck shoes have become the out-of-school uniform. At first it was difficult to spot him among the gaggle of schoolboys crowding the streets—he was just another one among a sea of faces. But as he's become older, shot up in height, and started to develop into a handsome young man, it's become easier for tourists and the paparazzi to identify him and point their cameras—something he hates.

Even official photographs are torture for him. During one photo call in 1994, while on a Mediterranean cruise with his father, he only agreed to pose after an argument with Prince Charles. A year later, he protested when photographers hounded

his mother, brother, and himself during a skiing holiday in Austria. And anyone who thinks he was relaxed and happy in photographs taken at Balmoral in 1997, when his budding heartthrob potential was starting to be noticed, can think again. Roll after roll of film was wasted, as the prince simply stared sullenly at his feet. Only a handful of shots showing a smiling, attractive youth were usable.

William's obvious attractiveness to girls was first seen at the Toffs Ball—the annual dance event on London's social calendar for rich kids—held in London's Hammersmith Palais. In October 1995, following his 13th birthday, William asked his parents if he could go with some of his Eton friends. Charles was against the idea, but was eventually persuaded to give his permission.

William turned up with some friends from Eton and the inevitable bodyguard, whose presence proved invaluable in keeping at bay the hordes of girls who asked the blushing young prince for a kiss. William knew better than to even think about it, but the attention must have been flattering. Since then he has been seen chatting to girls on the ski slopes, and is reported to have charmed many schoolmates' sisters. But serious dating? He has been out on dates, mostly arranged by his companions at Eton, but it must be difficult when your personal detective is lurking in the background!

The Prince and Princess of Wales divorced in August 1996. In the months that followed, Diana grew close to Dodi Fayed, the son of multimillionaire Mohamed al-Fayed, who owns Harrods, London's great department store. In the summer of 1997, the Fayeds invited Diana and her sons to their villa near St. Tropez, in the South of France. Despite the prying eyes of the paparazzi, William had an enjoyable time, especially when Dodi hired St. Tropez's most exclusive discotheque for the night for a private party. Wills and Harry really let their hair down.

When the holiday was over, William and Harry returned to London and then went on to Balmoral, where William had come to really enjoy the country pursuits his father loved so much. On September 1, 1997, at two o'clock in the morning, Prince Charles was woken to be told that Princess Diana had been involved in a serious car crash in Paris, and that Dodi Fayed and the driver had been killed. An hour later, news came through that Diana had died in a Paris hospital. Charles decided to let his sons sleep, then break the news to them when they woke up.

oth boys were devastated. When Tiggy Legge-Bourke heard the news, she flew to Balmoral to help comfort them. But even before she arrived, William and Harry had shown incredible composure as they accompanied their father and other members of the Royal Family to an eleven o'clock church service.

The days that followed were a nightmare for everyone. Both boys, so calm in public, would break down in tears at any time as the tragedy engulfed them. But when Charles flew to Paris immediately after the service, to escort Diana's body home, Wills seemed to instinctively realize that it was up to him to keep Harry occupied, to help keep his little brother's mind off the awful tragedy. He decided what games they should play, when to kick a ball around or go for a walk.

When Tiggy arrived, she took over this comforting role, and when Charles returned to Balmoral, he and William spent a lot of time together, chatting quietly indoors, fishing, or going for long walks on the estate. Sometimes they would talk about Diana's funeral, which Charles wanted both his sons to be involved in.

William

William knew his mother would not have wanted a very formal funeral. He was pleased when pop star Elton John agreed to sing a special version of *Candle in the Wind*, a song he had originally written in memory of the 1950s screen goddess Marilyn Monroe. He was also pleased when representatives of the charities Diana had been associated with were invited to walk, dressed informally, behind the coffin from Kensington Palace to Westminster Abbey. And he was relieved when the Queen said that this was to be "a unique funeral for a unique person."

When he wasn't with his father or Tiggy and Harry, William sat glued to the television, watching the amazing outpouring of public grief that erupted after Diana's death. As the bunches of flowers bloomed into floral walls around Buckingham Palace, St. James's Palace (where people stood in line for hours to sign books of condolence) and especially at Kensington Palace, he came to

understand just how deeply his mother had been loved. William also came to believe that the paparazzi had been responsible for her death. When he heard Diana's brother, Earl Spencer, who lived in South Africa, read out a statement saying that he believed the press had killed his sister, William cheered at the television.

On the morning of the funeral, Prince Charles asked his sons if they wanted to accompany him, Prince Philip, and Earl Spencer, and join the funeral procession at St. James's Palace. The boys agreed.

We will never know what was in William's mind as he took his place between his grandfather and uncle, and walked, head bowed, from the palace to Westminster Abbey. We will never know how he felt as he sat in Westminster Abbey listening to Elton John and others singing in tribute to Diana. We will never know what was going through his head as he listened to Earl Spencer's speech. We do know that, although he knew it was not proper to applaud at funerals, he smiled as he joined the 2,500 other mourners in the abbey in the storm of clapping that swept through the church after the earl had finished.

After the funeral and Diana's burial at Althorp, her family home in Northamptonshire, Charles took William and Harry to Highgrove, where he continued to help them come to terms with what had happened. Then it was time to return to school, where William's friends had been told that, after saying how sorry they were about Diana's death, they were never to mention the matter.

*I*t was a relief for William to be back with his friends. Although he felt guilty about being separated from Harry, who was now in his last year at Ludgrove before joining him at Eton in 1998, the two talked on the telephone for as long and as often as they wanted to.

William enjoys Eton. He is a hard worker who has already passed nine GCSEs (England's General Certificate of Secondary Education exams) with excellent grades, and has forged several strong friendships with boys who treat him no differently from anyone else. He is also close to Princess Anne's daughter Zara, and Prince Michael of Kent's daughter Lady Gabriella Windsor.

It is the relationships with his father, one that has deepened hugely since Diana died, and his brother that are the most important to him. He has also met Camilla Parker Bowles for the first time, in 1998—something his father would never have allowed when Diana was alive. Officially the two met by accident at St. James's Palace, when Wills dropped in to change clothes before going out for the evening, but it is said that William knew she would be there, and wanted to meet her so he could invite her to a surprise 50th birthday party he and Harry were throwing for their father at Highgrove. William was furious when the secret got out and was reported in the press.

Overall the press have respected requests to back off and let William enjoy as normal a life as possible for someone who is second in line to the throne. But given that he is the son of the most photographed woman in the world, and has inherited her looks and temperament, there is no doubt that William Arthur Philip Louis Mountbatten-Windsor is destined to become one of the world's most photographed men.

Prince William